An Entertaining Guide to Basic Accounting

by Bart Cecere

Illustrations by Rich Rice

T0182782

DORRANCE
PUBLISHING CO
EST. 1920
PITTSBURGH, PENNSYLVANIA 15238

The contents of this work, including, but not limited to, the accuracy of events, people, and places depicted; opinions expressed; permission to use previously published materials included; and any advice given or actions advocated are solely the responsibility of the author, who assumes all liability for said work and indemnifies the publisher against any claims stemming from publication of the work.

Dorrance Publishing Co
585 Alpha Drive
Suite 103
Pittsburgh, PA 15238
Visit our website at *www.dorrancebookstore.com*

ISBN: 978-1-6470-2210-5
eISBN: 978-1-6470-2911-1

It had been well-known that the founder of the double-entry accounting (bookkeeping) system was in 1494 by a Franciscan monk from Milan by the name of Luca Pagioli.

This was refuted, claiming that the actual founder was a Croatian, in 1416, by the name of Benedikt Kotruljevic.

Who knows? But whoever was responsible, the method is ingenious in its simplicity.

To my readers:

I was an accountant with a private practice. In my earlier years of practicing I had the opportunity to teach "Financial Accounting" (basics) at Rutgers University over a period of five years. During this term, I realized that those students who were to continue on in this major may not have grasped the basics. This would make their lives much more difficult, and even those students merely experiencing basic accounting and moving on to other endeavors would benefit from an understanding of the mechanics and use of this subject.

This book, having its major purpose in clarifying basics to high school seniors and college freshmen, will also benefit the rest. Every business or other organization will inevitably expose you to some form of accounting, perhaps in the form of financial statements. Every small or large business, charitable organization, homeowners' association, etc., will require its participants to read and understand balance sheets and profit and loss statements. So, to the non-accountant: this book should help you, too.

Following are examples of how non-accountant business people handled the accountant's product.

-Bart Cecere, CPA (Ret.)

Introduction

This is a book about accounting, not that any of you are interested in accounting, per se, but what you might be interested in is how it affects you or your business, and more specifically, how can an accountant be of value to you? How can what he does be of value to you?

I asked myself these questions, and some of the answers resulted in this book.

I'm an accountant, a CPA, previously with a private practice. (I will use the words accountant and CPA interchangeably.) CPA, or certified public accountant, doesn't actually tell you what I did, so to keep it simple, an account-ant accounts for things, and a CPA is a further earned title.

The fact that the designation of CPA isn't clear is the beginning of the prob-lem. I began looking more clearly at what I have been doing to make a living. In more basic terms, what do I give to people that they really want to have, for which I expect them to pay me? It turned out that this wasn't really easy to answer.

Placing myself in the shoes of a typical client, I tended to look at my ac-countant as a dull type of guy, who I had to see eventually (like that inevitable trip to the dentist, for the too long-awaited root canal.) As Mr. Typical Client, I hate to admit it, but I'm scared to death of the IRS, and my accountant makes the pain go away for a while… sometimes.

But otherwise, he speaks of lofty things and hands me a lot of papers with numbers on them that I don't understand. He asks me to sign a lot of papers, and for the most part, when I can be honest with myself, I don't really know what he is doing with all the records that I give him.

To add insult to injury, he always gives me a big bill.

So, here's the scenario:

A typical business owner thinks he needs to have an accountant, thinks he has to have reports (maybe the bank wants them), and is afraid to face IRS on this own, so he hires an accountant, but he really doesn't understand what the accountant is doing.

Some clients are a little less sensitive and will throw them in with the rest of the junk mail. Or, here's a good one—several clients put them in a folder marked "Accountant," and who do you think gets the contents of the folder next month?

Some clients are embarrassed that all this paper is being wasted on them and say things like, "Whaddya wasting all this paper for?"

This is my product, or at least I thought it was. This is where I spend a good deal of my time, and it results in something that someone doesn't understand. Because they don't know what it is.

But it's not their fault. It's mine. More correctly, it's ours. The CPAs and the accountants, because we produce this wonderful product that no one uses and no one understands.

I concluded that if I could change this, I could enhance my income potential, and at the same time do something for mankind. The result would be that my clients, and potential new clients, would be looking forward to next month's financial statement.

JUST IMAGINE BEING EXCITED ABOUT RECEIVING A FINANCIAL STATEMENT!

After some considerable thought, I knew that, if I could convince the average business person to sit still for two hours listening to an accountant talk about accounting, I could create a new interest and create a greater demand for the product and a necessary understanding of us.

This book's manual is being presented at the most basic introductory level. It assumes that the attendee either knows nothing of the subject or thinks he or she knows something and is willing to forget it all.

There are three major parts:

PART 1: Here we are going to take the most commonly used terms in accounting, used either in the mechanics (the books) or in the financial statements, and learn once and for all what they mean.

PART 2: Here you will see how a basic transaction such as a written check, a sale, or a collection works its way into the books, into the accounting (or bookkeeping system), and how it is finally reflected in the financial statement.

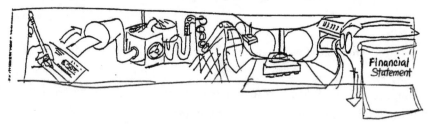

In a recent survey I did with business owners, amongst other questions, about one half of the respondents admitted to not understanding the reports they received from their accountants, and most of those that said they did understand, modified their answers with "MOSTLY," "SOMEWHAT," and "SO-SO".

HERE'S THE HEART OF THE PROBLEM: The accounting profession, not unlike the medical profession, has isolated itself from everyone else by developing a nomenclature*, that, at best, only accountants could understand.

*NOMENCLATURE – Webster's New Collegiate Dictionary, definition: (a) a system or set of terms or symbols; (b) a system of terms used in a particular science, discipline, or art

This is particularly true when the "BIG 8" or "BIG 6," whatever they are now called, report on a New York stock exchange company. Does anyone really understand these reports? The footnotes on earnings per share, pension costs, etc.? I doubt it!

And so, it is true on a smaller scale here with us, in the world of the small- and medium-sized businesses.

Now, going one step further, this accounting nomenclature, as we look at it more closely, begins to appear even more devious than that of the medical profession. The medical profession uses long, hard-to-pronounce Latin terms that most people, right off, won't even touch.

The accounting profession lures everyone in by using common, friendly, everyday words in their terms—so, "Of course I understand this, it's a BALANCE SHEET," "It's a FINANCIAL STATEMENT."

SO...

He can't be feeling wonderful when he pays the accountant's bill.

BECAUSE...

He doesn't feel as if he's getting something of value.

WHAT IS REALLY GOING ON HERE?

It's very, very true that accountants can and should help their clients a lot more by extending beyond the conventional reporting and tax return preparation, but that is a subject for another day.

Shouldn't these business owners, recipients of these fancy reports, understand them?

WELL, I DON'T THINK THEY DO!

It's just not true. At the risk of losing all my clients in one sentence, I'm going to make a very bold statement:

NOT ONE SINGLE CLIENT READS, COMPREHENDS, AND USES THE FINANCIAL STATEMENTS THAT I PREPARE REGULARLY!

How do I know? I know by their reactions.

Some clients are very polite and pretend to be reading them, if in my presence. Their manner will range from austere to quizzical, to surprised. In these instances, they sometimes take great issue with significances, such as a dollar sign. But they're just acting.

PART 3: Once a person understands the terms (nomenclature) and has a comprehension of the flow of the transaction (i.e. a written check, a sale, etc.)

through the accounting process, the reading of the basic financial statement (balance sheets, statement of earnings) and their relationship to each other, should be a brand-new experience.

ACCOUNTING NOMENCLATURE

FINANCIAL STATEMENT

A report that shows, in dollars, how a business, or other activity has done, and what its condition is.

HOW IT HAS DONE

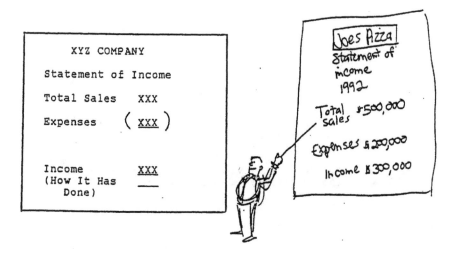

WHAT ITS CONDITION IS

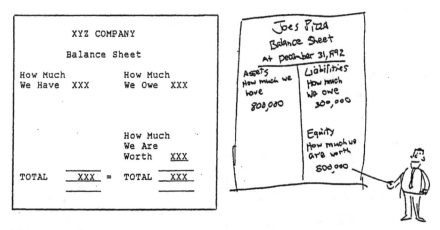

This report is often formal and reflects the summarized balances of accounts from the records of the business.

STATEMENT OF INCOME - or - INCOME STATEMENT

- or -

STATEMENT OF EARNINGS - or - PROFIT & LOSS

The financial statement that shows, in dollars, how a business, or other activity, has done FOR A SPECIFIC PERIOD OF TIME.

XYZ COMPANY

Statement of Income

For The Year Ended
December 31, 19XX

TOTAL SALES	XXX
EXPENSES	XXX
INCOME	XXX

BALANCE SHEET - or - STATEMENT OF CONDITION

or

STATEMENT OF FINANCIAL CONDITION

The financial statement that shows, in dollars, the condition of a business, or other activity, <u>AS OF A SPECIFIC DATE</u>.

```
                    XYZ COMPANY

                   Balance Sheet

              (AT) December 31, 19XX

          ASSETS                LIABILITIES


     HOW MUCH                 HOW MUCH
     WE HAVE                  WE OWE

               XXX                        XXX




                              EQUITY
                              HOW MUCH WE
                              ARE WORTH    XXX

     TOTAL     XXX            TOTAL        XXX
```

ASSET (AN ACCOUNT)

An item of value on a balance sheet. It could be liquid cash, something physically owned, something done or paid for that gives a certain right to something. (Assets appear on the left side of the balance sheet.)

EXAMPLES OF ASSET ACCOUNTS

Cash in bank

Inventory

Accounts receivable

Furniture, auto, etc.

Prepaid insurance

Trademark

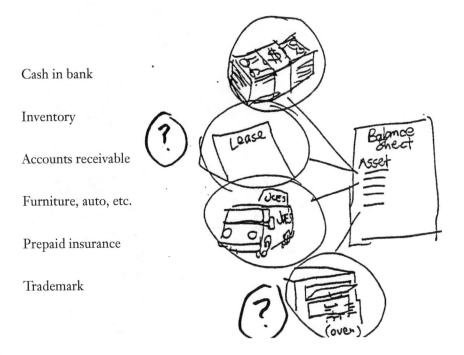

LIABILITY (AN ACCOUNT)

An item that shows what is owed, either in money or performance of service. (Liabilities appear on the right side of the balance sheet.)

EXAMPLES OF LIABILITY ACCOUNTS

Accounts payable

Notes or loans payable

Payroll taxes payable

*Accrued expenses payable ("matching" revenues & expenses)

Deferred income (advance payments)

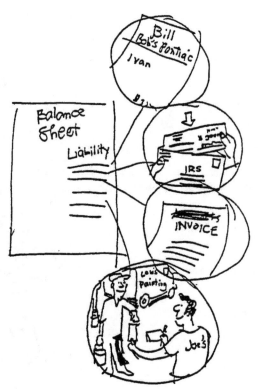

EQUITY (AN ACCOUNT) - or - CAPITAL (AN ACCOUNT)
(SOMETIMES CALLED NET WORTH)

The excess of assets over liabilities. (We call it a <u>DEFICIT</u> when there is an excess of liabilities over assets.)

Equity accounts appear on the right side of the balance sheet.
Equity (accounts) consist of:

In a corporation:

A. Capital stock or preferred stock and common stock
B. Retained earnings

In a proprietorship or partnership:

A. Capital, or owner's equity, or partners' capital

REVENUES (AN ACCOUNT)

Items appearing in statement of income that represent <u>GROSS</u> income, or <u>GROSS</u> billings, e.g. <u>SALES</u>, <u>REVENUES</u>.

```
                    XYZ COMPANY


                Statement of Income

                For the year ended


                December 31, 19xx


    SALES                              XXX
```

COST OF GOODS SOLD/COST OF SALES (AN ACCOUNT)

The items of cost, or expense, appearing in statements of income that show total costs <u>DIRECTLY</u> related to the total of sales or revenues.

Generally this includes, but is not limited to, the cost of materials (inventory) that has been sold.

```
          XYZ COMPANY

       Statement of Income

        For the Year Ended

        December 31, 19XX


  SALES                        XXX


  COST OF SALES                XXX


  GROSS PROFIT                 XXX
```

GROSS PROFIT (NOT AN ACCOUNT, JUST A SUB TOTAL)

The net result, or difference between sales and cost of sales, sometimes called "margin" or "gross margin."

```
            XYZ COMPANY

        Statement of Income

         For the Year Ended

         December 31, 19XX


    SALES                    XXX


    COST OF SALES            XXX


    GROSS PROFIT             XXX
```

EXPENSE (AN ACCOUNT)

Bills paid or incurred for the period, reflected in the statement of income.

Examples of Expense Accounts

Rent

Salaries

Telephone

Taxes

Office expense

Accounting fees

```
        XYZ COMPANY

     Statement of Income
      For the Year Ended
      December 31, 19XX

SALES                  XXX
COST OF SALES          XXX
GROSS PROFIT           XXX

EXPENSES               XXX
```

CURRENT ASSETS (GROUP OF ACCOUNTS)

Those assets that are either liquid (are cash or can be converted to cash), such as cash in bank, or are expected to become liquid within one (1) year.

Examples of Current Asset Accounts

Cash in bank

Inventories

Accounts receivable

Notes receivable (if due in one year)

Prepaid expense, such as insurance, taxes, etc.

CURRENT LIABILITIES (GROUP OF ACCOUNTS)

Those liabilities, debts, or obligations that are expected to be paid or otherwise satisfied within one (1) year.

Examples of Current Liabilities
Accounts payable
Notes payable (due within one year)
Deferred income

DEBIT

Accounting entry made on the left side of the ledger. (HAS NO OTHER MEANING!)

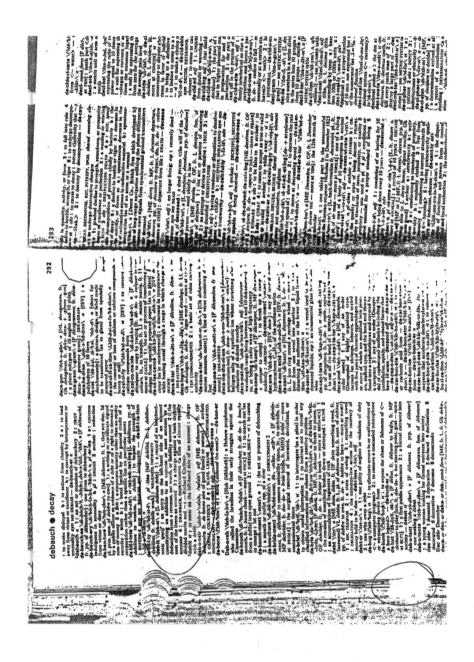

CREDIT

Accounting entry made on the right side of the ledger.

A **CREDIT** IS AN **ENTRY** MADE ON the **RIGHT** side of the ledger NOTHING ELSE !!!

A CREDIT IS AN ENTRY MADE ON THE RIGHT SIDE OF THE LEDGER

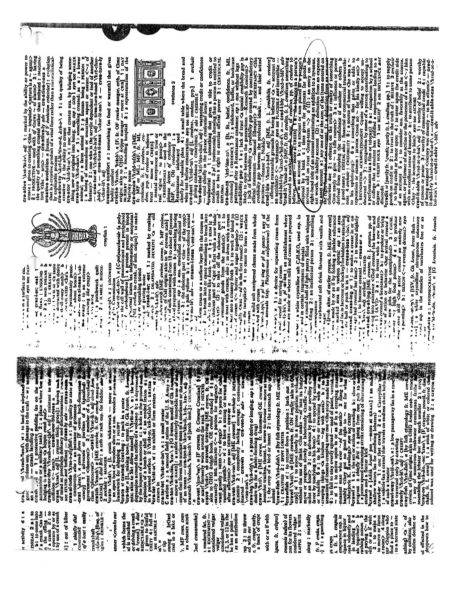

MECHANICS OF ACCOUNTING

MECHANICS OF ACCOUNTING

THE ACCOUNTING EQUATION

Why is a balance sheet called a balance sheet?

Here's proof that accountants were not thinking about the reader when they named this:

The term "balance sheet" more closely relates to the "mechanics" of accounting than it does to the value or use of the statement.

LOOK AT THIS

SOME TYPICAL TRANSACTIONS

These entries will always be true to the accounting equation and always will follow the DEBIT/CREDIT rules.

Every business transaction that has a dollar amount needs an accounting entry, and every entry affects the accounting equation.

ASSETS = LIABILITIES + EQUITY

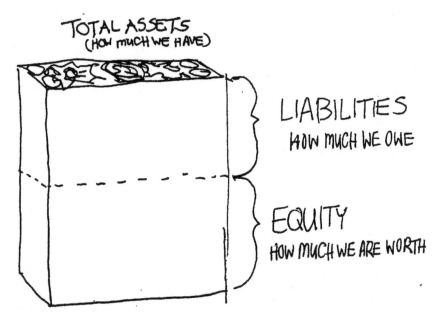

The balance sheet <u>balances</u>.

Every entry in accounting <u>balances</u>.

When a debit entry is made, a credit entry must be made. This is what's called the <u>DOUBLE ENTRY SYSTEM.</u>

Simple Illustration:

ASSETS	LIABILITIES	EQUITY
Business has $200 in the bank.	It owes $50	It is worth $150

Business has
$200 in the bank (assets)

It owes $50
(liabilities)

It is worth
$150
(equity)

$150	$150
Into bank account.	Value.

ASSETS	LIABILITIES	EQUITY
$150 in bank.		$150 in bank

So, there's a $150 value.
BORROWS $50.

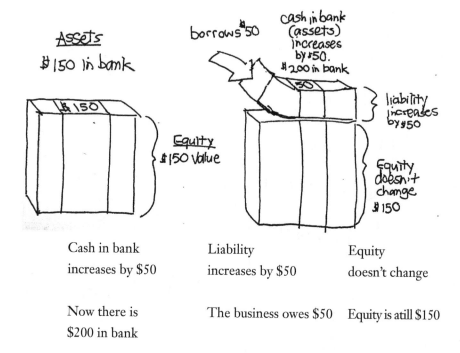

Cash in bank increases by $50	Liability increases by $50	Equity doesn't change
Now there is $200 in bank	The business owes $50	Equity is atill $150

Example 1

Write a check to buy a desk for $500.

How it affects the accounting equation:

One asset, cash in bank, is reduced by $500, and another asset, furniture, is increased by $500.

ASSET	LIABILITY	EQUITY
Increases $500	No change	No change
Decreases $500		

Example 2

Collect a $250 accounts receivable.

ASSETS	LIABILITIES	EQUITY
Increases cash by $250.	No Change.	No Change.
Decreases account receivables by $250.		

Example 3

Pay an accounts payable for $300.

ASSET
Reduce cash by $300.

LIABILITY
Reduce accounts
payable by $300.

EQUITY
No Change

Example 4

Borrow $1,000 from the bank.

ASSET	LIABILITY	EQUITY
Increase cash by $1,000.	Increase note payable by $1,000.	No Change

Example 5

Collect a deposit of $450 in advance from a customer.

ASSET	LIABILITY	EQUITY
Increase cash by $450	Increase deferred income by $450	No Change

(We have not <u>earned</u> this yet because we have not performed the service, and therefore, we <u>owe</u> something.)

Example 6

Invest $2000 in a business.

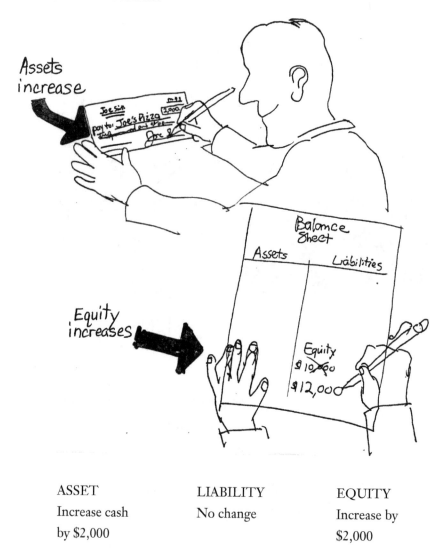

ASSET	LIABILITY	EQUITY
Increase cash by $2,000	No change	Increase by $2,000

You might have noticed that we have not shown entries that reflect income, expense, revenue, profit, and loss.

It is important now, that we look into the deep dark intimacies of the accounting mechanics.

Here, we must face the DEBIT and the CREDIT.

For every transaction, there must be an entry made

A) on the left,

and

B) on the right.

To make sense of the interplay between assets, liabilities, equity, revenues and costs, and expenses, a system had to be formulated to do this mechanically, so it always came out right.

In one entry:

A. Two accounts can increase

B. Two accounts can decrease

C. One account can increase while one decreases.

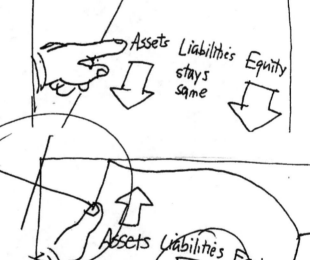

This is why we need

DEBITS AND CREDITS.

Debit	Credit
Entry made on left	Entry made on right

But first, let's show how revenues, costs, and expenses affect the accounting equation.

REMEMBER: ASSETS = LIABILITIES + EQUITY

WHERE ARE THE REVENUES, COSTS, AND EXPENSES?

When a revenue is earned or, in more common terms, when a business makes money, it increases in equity!

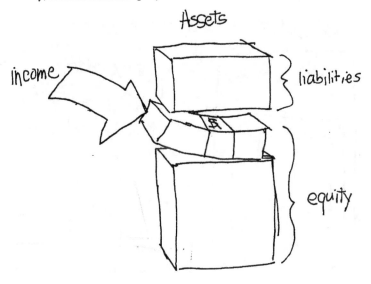

When a cost or expense is incurred or, more commonly, when a business spends money (on an expense consumed, not on another asset), IT DE-CREASES IN EQUITY.

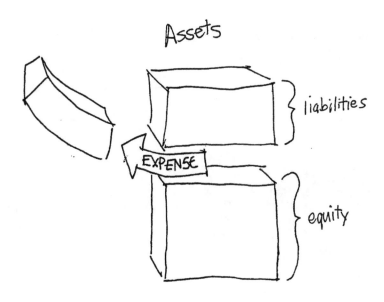

Spending on another asset, for instance a desk, does not change how much you are worth – equity.

VERY SIMPLY, IF WE GO BACK TO THE EQUATION:

ASSETS = LIABILITIES + EQUITY

A business makes money (earns revenue, makes a profit), <u>equity increases.</u>

Increase in assets, has more cash, has accounts receivable, etc.

An increase on both sides of equation.

ALSO –

ASSETS = LIABILITIES + EQUITY

A business pays its rent, <u>equity decreases.</u>

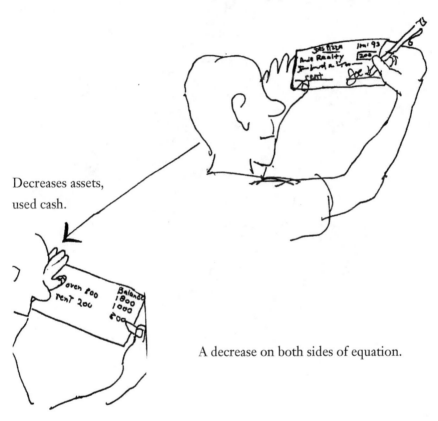

Decreases assets,
used cash.

A decrease on both sides of equation.

AND –

ASSETS = LIABILITIES + EQUITY

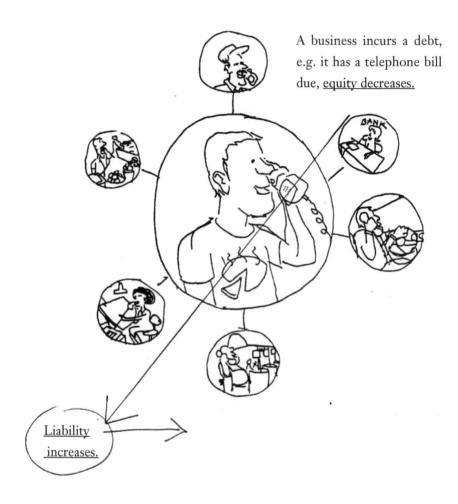

A business incurs a debt, e.g. it has a telephone bill due, <u>equity decreases.</u>

Liability increases.

An increase and a decrease on same side of equation.

Here is a general ledger account (see glossary):

Debit	Credit
Left Side	Right Side

There is a general ledger account for every asset, liability, equity, revenue, cost and expense account, and the rules are always the same.

EXPANDED EQUATION

ASSETS = LIABILITIES + EQUITY

ASSETS = LIABILITIES + (OWNER'S INVESTMENT IN THE BUSINESS) + (REVENUE-EXPENSES)

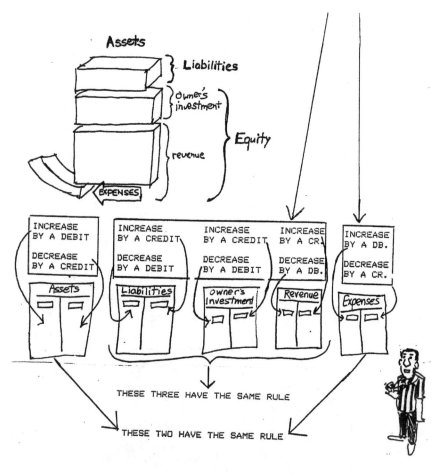

ENTRY 1

Started a business; invested $1,000.

CASH IN BANK:

$1,000

COMMON STOCK:

$1,000

ENTRY 2

Bought office furniture for $500.

FURNITURE:

$500

CASH IN BANK:

$500

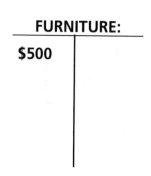

ENTRY 3

Bought a computer for $900, but didn't pay for it yet.

COMPUTER:

$900

ACCOUNTS PAYABLE:

$900

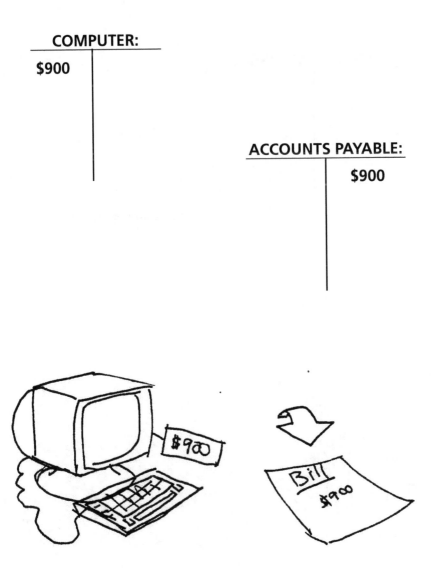

ENTRY 4

Sold services for $1,200, but didn't collect it.

ACCOUNTS RECEIVABLE:

$1,200

REVENUES (SALES):

$1,200

ENTRY 5

Paid a sub-contractor to help perform services $250.

SUB CONTRACTOR EXPENSE:

$250

CASH IN BANK:

$250

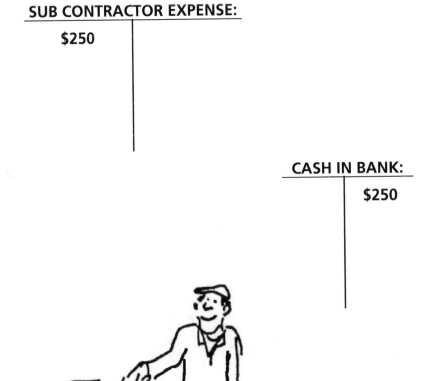

ENTRY 6

Collected one-half of accounts receivable.

CASH IN BANK:

$600

ACCOUNTS RECEIVABLE:

$600

ENTRY 7

Made a partial payment on computer of $450.

ACCOUNTS PAYABLE:

$450

CASH IN BANK:

$450

ENTRY 8

Borrowed $2,500 from the bank.

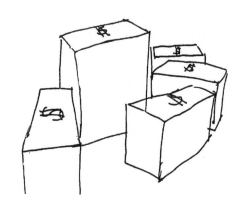

CASH IN BANK:

$2,500

BANK LOAN PAYABLE:

$2,500

CASH IN BANK:

1. 1,000	2. 500
6. 600	5. 250
8. 2,500	7. 450
4100	1200

Bal. $2,900

FURNITURE:

2. 500	

Bal. $2,900

ACCOUNTS PAYABLE:

7. 450	3. 900

Bal. $2,900

COMMON STOCK:

	1. 1,000

Bal. $1,000

ACCOUNTS | RECEIVABLE:

4. 1,200	6. 600

Bal. $600

Bob's Renos
Bill

painting   1200
less payment   600

balance due 600

COMPUTER:

3. 900	

Bal. 900

BANK LOAN PAYABLE:

8. $2,500

Bal. $600

REVENUES:

4. 1,200

Bal. $1.200

SUB CONTRACTOR EXPENSES:

5. $250

Bal. $250

Effect of the above entries in the accounting equation.

ENTRY	ASSETS	=	LIABILITIES	+	EQUITY
1	$1000				$1,000
2	$500				
	($500)				
3	$900		$900		
4	$1,200				$1,200
5	($250)				($250)
6	$600				
	($600)				
7	($450)		($450)		
8	$2,500		$2,500		
	$4,900		**$2,950**		**$1,950**

While we are in the equation, we can use plusses and minuses, not debits and credits.

At the end of an accounting period, for mechanics only, all of the revenue accounts (they would have credit balances) and all of the cost and expense accounts (they would have debit balances) would be placed into an equity account:

1) In a corporation this would be called retained earnings
2) In a proprietorship or a partnership this would be called capital.

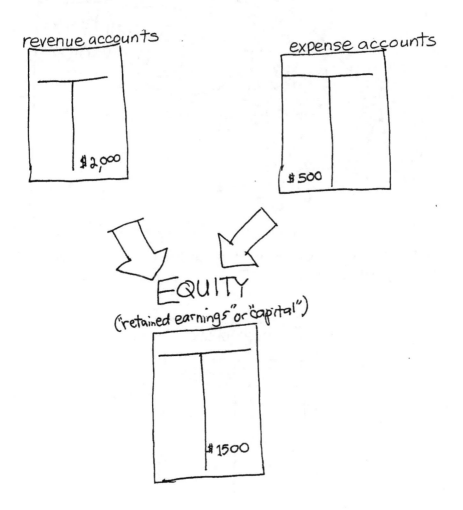

revenue accounts

$2,000

expense accounts

$500

EQUITY
("retained earnings" or "capital")

$1500

Understand that, in actuality, e.g. when an asset increases,

the corresponding increase in the revenue account immediately increases the equity in the equation.

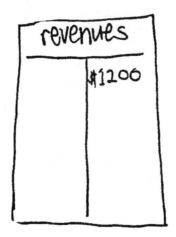

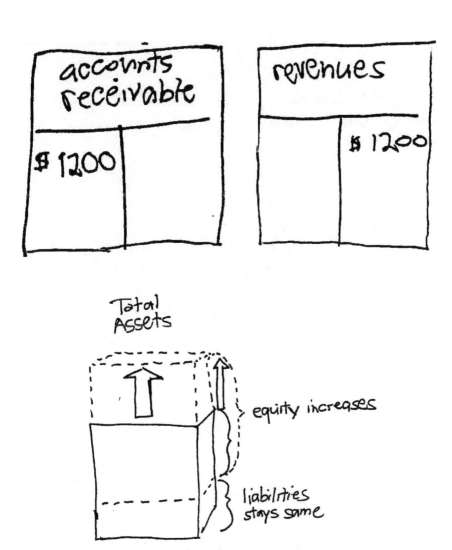

The mechanics of transferring the results of this to retained earnings so that the financial statements can be prepared is a "catch up" to reflect this.

This balance sheet would look like this without it.

ASSETS		LIABILITIES	
CASH IN BANK	$2,900	ACCOUNTS PAYABLE	$450
ACCOUNTS RECEIVABLE	$600	BANK LOAN PAYABLE	$2,500
TOTAL CURRENT ASSETS	$3,500	TOTAL CURRENT LIABILITIES	$2,950
FURNITURE AND FIXTURES	$1,400	STOCKHOLDER'S EQUITY COMMON STOCK	$1,000
TOTAL ASSETS	$4,900		

What is missing?

Revenues of $1,200 <u>increased</u> equity.

Sub-contractor expenses of $250 <u>decreased</u> equity.

The statement of income would show:

XYZ COMPANY

Statement of Income
Month of January 19XX

Revenues	$1200
Expenses Sub-Contractor	$250
Net Income	$950

CONCLUSIONS

SUMMARY

(This is called a "Trial Balance")

ACCOUNT	BALANCE	
	DEBIT	CREDIT
CASH IN BANK	$2,900	
ACCOUNTS RECEIVABLE	$600	
FURNITURE	$500	
COMPUTER	$900	
ACCOUNTS PAYABLE		$450
BANK LOAN PAYABLE		$2,500
COMMON STOCK		$1,000
REVENUES		$1,200
SUB CONTRACTOR EXPENSES	$250	
	$5,150	$5,150

Everything still balances.

We followed the accounting equation <u>and</u> the Debit/Credit rules.

The accounts would be "closed" as follows:

REVENUES:	
A. $1,200 Entry to close	Bal. $1,200

Balance -0-

SUB CONTRACTOR EXPENSES:	
Bal. $250	A. $250 Entry to close

Balance -0-

RETAINED EARNINGS:	
2. $250	A. $950 Entry to close
	1. $1,200

Balance -0-

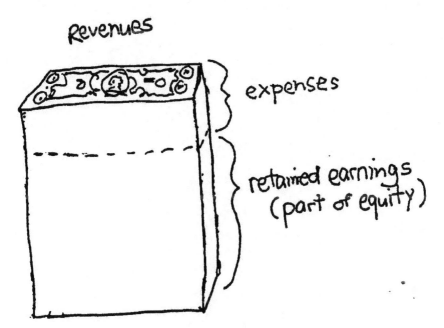

Revenues

expenses

retained earnings
(part of equity)

Go back four pages and complete the balance sheet...

We'll just put in the revenues and expenses... reeevv eennuue aaannd exxpeeeennsess...

The retained earnings account of a corporation would then be equal to, from period to period or from year to year, the total accumulation of <u>all</u> net income, or net losses, from the inception of the business to the present time, net of any dividends paid.

In a proprietorship or a partnership, the account would be called "capital" and would also represent the accumulation of income and losses, plus monies invested, less monies drawn out.

READING FINANCIAL STATEMENTS

So, the relationship between the two basic financial statements, i.e., the balance sheet and the statement of income, becomes evident.

The balance sheet reflects the present amounts of assets, liabilities, and equities, which balances have been increased or decreased by...

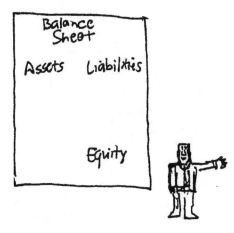

1) Items not reflected in the income statement, such as:

   a) Investment in the business.

   b) Collections of accounts receivable

   c) Payments of accounts payable

d) Borrowing

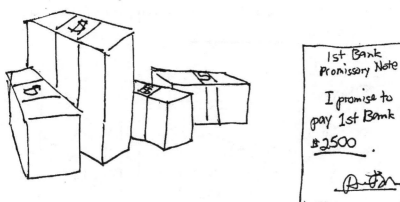

2) Items reflected in the income statements, such as:

a) Realization of revenues (sales)

b) Expenses incurred

Equity consists of:

1) What was invested in the business; in a corporation, this is reflected as common stock.

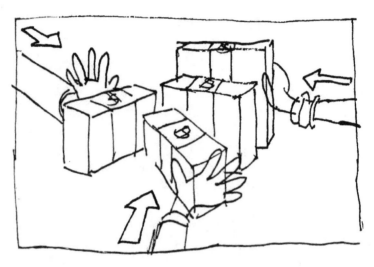

2) The increase in value of the business through profits (income).

Equity will always equal the excess of assets over liabilities:

a) See the accounting equation

b) See the balance sheet

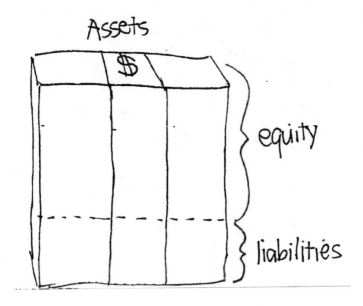

Every time money is invested in the business and each time a profit is made, net assets increase.

Let's review your financial statements.

APPENDIX I

GLOSSARY OF TERMS:

ACCOUNTS: Those classifications within a business's books i.e., general ledger, which reflect the balances resulting from monetary activity.

GENERAL LEDGER: The standard bookkeeping record from which financial statements are prepared, which reflects the cumulative balances or totals throughout the accounting year of all the business's accounts.

Examples of accounts:

Cash in the Bank	Balance at a Date
Accounts receivable	
Furniture	
Accounts Payable	
Revenues (Sales)	Total to Date
Telephone Expense	
Rent Expense	

JOURNAL ENTRY: The accountant's way of entering financial transactions into a general ledger.

ACCRUAL: A type of journal entry which records an item that has happened but hasn't been paid; i.e. billing a customer, but not yet getting paid, or receiving a telephone bill, but not yet paying it.

ACCRUED EXPENSE: Generally a liability that has been recorded and reflected in the balance sheet to show that an item of expense belongs in the current period, but has not yet been paid.

NET ASSETS: Assets minus liabilities (same as equity).

INCUR, AS IN TO INCUR AN EXPENSE: To become liable for a debt.

LIQUID: According to Webster's, consisting of or capable of ready conversion into cash.

PROPRIETORSHIP: A business owned by a single person.

PARTNERSHIP: A business owned by two or more persons under a partnership agreement.

CORPORATION: A business whose ownership is evidenced by shares of stock.

APPENDIX II

SOME ITEMS NOT COVERED IN THIS SEMINAR:

- Depreciation
- Compilations, reviews, and audits
- Statement of retained earnings
- Changes in working capital
- Changes in cash flow
- Budgets, forecasts, and projections
- Long term debt
- Income taxes
- Financial statement ratios
- Accounting for inventories

Printed in the USA
CPSIA information can be obtained
at www.ICGtesting.com
LVHW011117310724
786976LV00002B/253